Angular Router

From Angular core team member and creator of the router

Victor Savkin

BIRMINGHAM - MUMBAI

Angular Router

First published: March 2017

Production reference: 2070317

Published by Packt Publishing Ltd.
Livery Place
35 Livery Street
Birmingham
B3 2PB, UK.
ISBN 978-1-78728-890-4

www.packtpub.com

Credits

Author

Victor Savkin

Acquisition Editor

Ben Renow-Clarke

Indexer

Aishwarya Gangawane

Technical Editor

Nidhisha Shetty

Production Coordinator

Shraddha Falebhai

About the Author

Victor Savkin has been on the Angular team since the inception of Angular 2. He developed dependency injection, change detection, forms, and the router.

Victor has worked for many years as a software architect helping to build large Angular applications. He gives talks and writes articles on front-end architectures for InfoQ, DZone, Hackerbits, and his blog.

Nrwl.io - Angular consulting for enterprise customers, from core team members

Victor is co-founder of Nrwl, a company providing Angular consulting for enterprise customers, from core team members. Visit **Nrwl** at `https://nrwl.io/` for more information.

www.PacktPub.com

For support files and downloads related to your book, please visit www.PacktPub.com.

Did you know that Packt offers eBook versions of every book published, with PDF and ePub files available? You can upgrade to the eBook version at www.PacktPub.com and as a print book customer, you are entitled to a discount on the eBook copy. Get in touch with us at service@packtpub.com for more details.

At www.PacktPub.com, you can also read a collection of free technical articles, sign up for a range of free newsletters and receive exclusive discounts and offers on Packt books and eBooks.

https://www.packtpub.com/mapt

Get the most in-demand software skills with Mapt. Mapt gives you full access to all Packt books and video courses, as well as industry-leading tools to help you plan your personal development and advance your career.

Why subscribe?

- Fully searchable across every book published by Packt
- Copy and paste, print, and bookmark content
- On demand and accessible via a web browser

Customer Feedback

Thanks for purchasing this Packt book. At Packt, quality is at the heart of our editorial process. To help us improve, please leave us an honest review on this book's Amazon page at `https://www.amazon.com/dp/1787288900`.

If you'd like to join our team of regular reviewers, you can e-mail us at `customerreviews@packtpub.com`. We award our regular reviewers with free eBooks and videos in exchange for their valuable feedback. Help us be relentless in improving our products!

Table of Contents

Preface

What this book covers

Managing state transitions is one of the hardest parts of building applications. This is especially true on the web, where you also need to ensure that the state is reflected in the URL. In addition, we often want to split applications into multiple bundles and load them on demand. Doing this transparently is not trivial.

The Angular router solves these problems. Using the router, you can declaratively specify application states, manage state transitions while taking care of the URL, and load bundles on demand.

In this book, I will talk about the router's mental model, its API, and the design principles behind it. To make one thing clear: this book is not about Angular. There is a lot of information about the framework available online. So if you want to get familiar with the framework first, I would recommend the following resources:

- `angular.io`: It's the best place to get started
- `egghead.io`: The Angular Fundamentals on `egghead.io` is an excellent way to get started for those who learn better by watching
- `vsavkin.com`: My blog contains many articles where I write about Angular in depth

Therefore in this book, I assume you are familiar with Angular, and so I won't talk about dependency injection, components, or bindings. I will only talk about the router.

Who this book is for

Why would you read this book if you can find the information about the router online?

This book goes far beyond a how-to-get-started guide. It is a complete description of the Angular router. The mental model, design constraints, and the subtleties of the API - everything is covered. Understanding these will give you deep insights into why the router works the way it does and will make you an Angular router expert.

Conventions

In this book, you will find a number of text styles that distinguish between different kinds of information. Here are some examples of these styles and an explanation of their meaning.

Code words in text, database table names, folder names, filenames, file extensions, path names, dummy URLs, user input, and Twitter handles are shown as follows: "Then, it will instantiate `ConversationCmp` with `MessagesCmp` in it, with `ComposeCmp` displayed as a popup."

A block of code is set as follows:

```
@Component({
  template: `
    Edit
  `
})
class MessageCmp {
  public id: string;
  constructor(private route: ActivatedRoute) {
    route.params.subscribe(_ => this.id = _.id);
  }
}
```

When we wish to draw your attention to a particular part of a code block, the relevant lines or items are set in bold:

```
@Component({
  template: `
    Edit
  `
})
class MessageCmp {
  public id: string;
  constructor(private route: ActivatedRoute) {
    route.params.subscribe(_ => this.id = _.id);
  }
}
```

New terms and **important words** are shown in bold. Words that you see on the screen, for example, in menus or dialog boxes, appear in the text like this: "In order to download new modules, we will go to **Files** | **Settings** | **Project Name** | **Project Interpreter**."

Warnings or important notes appear in a box like this.

Tips and tricks appear like this.

Reader feedback

Feedback from our readers is always welcome. Let us know what you think about this book-what you liked or disliked. Reader feedback is important for us as it helps us develop titles that you will really get the most out of. To send us general feedback, simply e-mail feedback@packtpub.com, and mention the book's title in the subject of your message. If there is a topic that you have expertise in and you are interested in either writing or contributing to a book, see our author guide at www.packtpub.com/authors.

Customer support

Now that you are the proud owner of a Packt book, we have a number of things to help you to get the most from your purchase.

Downloading the example code

You can download the example code files for this book from your account at http://www.packtpub.com. If you purchased this book elsewhere, you can visit http://www.packtpub.com/support and register to have the files e-mailed directly to you.

You can download the code files by following these steps:

1. Log in or register to our website using your e-mail address and password.
2. Hover the mouse pointer on the **SUPPORT** tab at the top.
3. Click on **Code Downloads & Errata**.
4. Enter the name of the book in the **Search** box.

5. Select the book for which you're looking to download the code files.
6. Choose from the drop-down menu where you purchased this book from.
7. Click on **Code Download**.

Once the file is downloaded, please make sure that you unzip or extract the folder using the latest version of:

- WinRAR / 7-Zip for Windows
- Zipeg / iZip / UnRarX for Mac
- 7-Zip / PeaZip for Linux

The code bundle for the book is also hosted on GitHub at `https://github.com/PacktPubl ishing/Angular-Router`. We also have other code bundles from our rich catalog of books and videos available at `https://github.com/PacktPublishing/`. Check them out!

Downloading the color images of this book

We also provide you with a PDF file that has color images of the screenshots/diagrams used in this book. The color images will help you better understand the changes in the output. You can download this file from `https://www.packtpub.com/sites/default/files/down loads/AngularRouter_ColorImages.pdf`.

Errata

Although we have taken every care to ensure the accuracy of our content, mistakes do happen. If you find a mistake in one of our books-maybe a mistake in the text or the code-we would be grateful if you could report this to us. By doing so, you can save other readers from frustration and help us improve subsequent versions of this book. If you find any errata, please report them by visiting `http://www.packtpub.com/submit-errata`, selecting your book, clicking on the **Errata Submission Form** link, and entering the details of your errata. Once your errata are verified, your submission will be accepted and the errata will be uploaded to our website or added to any list of existing errata under the Errata section of that title.

To view the previously submitted errata, go to `https://www.packtpub.com/books/conten t/support` and enter the name of the book in the search field. The required information will appear under the **Errata** section.

Piracy

Piracy of copyrighted material on the Internet is an ongoing problem across all media. At Packt, we take the protection of our copyright and licenses very seriously. If you come across any illegal copies of our works in any form on the Internet, please provide us with the location address or website name immediately so that we can pursue a remedy.

Please contact us at `copyright@packtpub.com` with a link to the suspected pirated material.

We appreciate your help in protecting our authors and our ability to bring you valuable content.

Questions

If you have a problem with any aspect of this book, you can contact us at `questions@packtpub.com`, and we will do our best to address the problem.

Example

For all the examples in this book we will use MailApp, which is an application akin to Inbox or Gmail. At launch, the application displays a list of conversations, which we can browse through. Once we click on a conversation, we can see all its messages. We can also compose a new message, or view an existing message in a popup.

You can find the source code of the MailApp application here: `https://github.com/vsavk in/router_mailapp`.

The code in this book has been simplified and altered in places to make it more appropriate for teaching. The final MailApp code on GitHub illustrates how this teaching code can be applied in a full application.

1

What Do Routers Do?

Before we jump into the specifics of the Angular router, let's talk about what routers do in general.

As you know, an Angular application is a tree of components. Some of these components are reusable UI components (for example, list and table), and some are application components, which represent screens or some logical parts of the application. The router cares about application components, or, to be more specific, about their arrangements. Let's call such component arrangements router states. So a router state defines what is visible on the screen.

 A router state is an arrangement of application components that defines what is visible on the screen.

Router configuration

The router configuration defines all the potential router states of the application. Let's look at an example:

```
[
  {
    path: ':folder',
    children: [
      {
        path: '',
        component: ConversationsCmp
      },
      {
        path: ':id',
```

```
            component: ConversationCmp,
            children: [
              { path: 'messages', component: MessagesCmp },
              { path: 'messages/:id', component: MessageCmp }
            ]
          }
        ]
      },
      {
        path: 'compose',
        component: ComposeCmp,
        outlet: 'popup'
      },
      {
        path: 'message/:id',
        component: PopupMessageCmp,
        outlet: 'popup'
      }
    ]
```

Don't worry about understanding all the details. I will cover them in later chapters. For now, let's depict the configuration as follows:

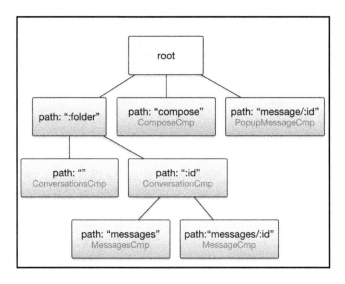

As you can see the router configuration is a tree, with every node representing a route. Some nodes have components associated with them, some do not. We also use color to designate different outlets, where an outlet is a location in the component tree where a component is placed.

Router state

A router state is a subtree of the configuration tree. For instance, the following example has ConversationsCmp activated. We say *activated* instead of *instantiated* as a component can be instantiated only once but activated multiple times (any time its route's parameters change):

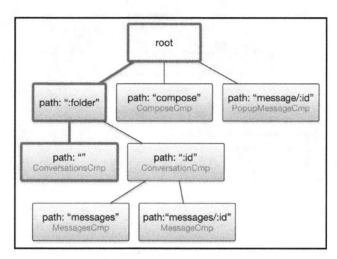

Not all subtrees of the configuration tree are valid router states. If a node has multiple children of the same color, that is, of the same outlet name, only one of them can be active at a time. For instance, ComposeCmp and PopupMessageCmp cannot be displayed together, but ConversationsCmp and PopupMessageCmp can. Stands to reason, an outlet is nothing but a location in the DOM where a component is placed. So we cannot place more than one component into the same location at the same time.

Navigation

The router's primary job is to manage navigation between states, which includes updating the component tree.

 Navigation is the act of transitioning from one router state to another.

To see how it works, let's look at the following example. Say we perform a navigation from the state preceding to this one:

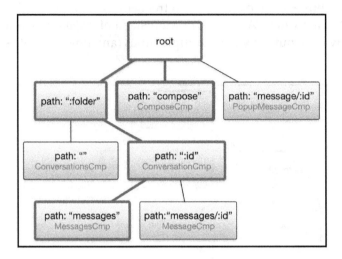

Because `ConversationsCmp` is no longer active, the router will remove it. Then, it will instantiate `ConversationCmp` with `MessagesCmp` in it, with `ComposeCmp` displayed as a popup.

Summary

That's it. The router simply allows us to express all the potential states which our application can be in, and provides a mechanism for navigating from one state to another. The devil, of course, is in the implementation details, but understanding this mental model is crucial for understanding the implementation.

Isn't it all about the URL?

The URL bar provides a huge advantage for web applications over native ones. It allows us to reference states, bookmark them, and share them with our friends. In a well-behaved web application, any application state transition results in a URL change, and any URL change results in a state transition. In other words, a URL is nothing but a serialized router state. The Angular router takes care of managing the URL to make sure that it is always in-sync with the router state.

2

Overview

Now that we have learned what routers do in general, it is time to talk about the Angular router.

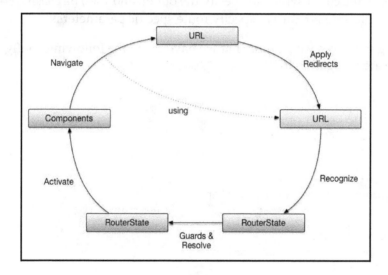

The Angular router takes a URL, then does the following:

1. Applying redirects.

2. Recognizing router states.

3. Running guards and resolving data.

4. Activating all the needed components.

5. Managing navigation.

Most of it happens behind the scenes, and, usually, we do not need to worry about it. But remember, the purpose of this book is to teach you how to configure the router to handle any crazy requirement your application might have. So let's get on it!

URL format

Since I will use a lot of URLs in the following examples, let's quickly look at the URL formats:

- `/inbox/33(popup:compose)`
- `/inbox/33;open=true/messages/44`

As you can see, the router uses parentheses to serialize secondary segments (for example, `popup:compose`), the colon syntax to specify the outlet, and the `;parameter=value` syntax (for example, `open=true`) to specify route specific parameters.

In the following examples we assume that we have given the following configuration to the router, and we are navigating to `/inbox/33/messages/44`:

```
[
  { path: '', pathMatch: 'full', redirectTo: '/inbox' },
  {
    path: ':folder',
    children: [
      {
        path: '',
        component: ConversationsCmp
      },
      {
        path: ':id',
        component: ConversationCmp,
        children: [
          { path: 'messages', component: MessagesCmp },
          { path: 'messages/:id', component: MessageCmp }
        ]
      }
    ]
  },
  {
    path: 'compose',
    component: ComposeCmp,
    outlet: 'popup'
  },
  {
```

```
    path: 'message/:id',
    component: PopupMessageCmp,
    outlet: 'popup'
  }
]
```

Applying redirects

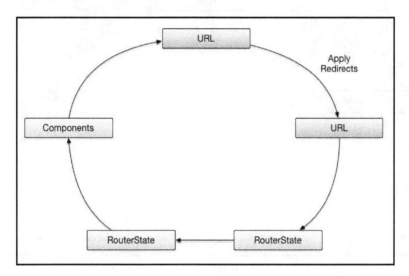

The router gets a URL from the user, either when she clicks on a link or updates the location bar directly. The first thing that router does with this URL is it will apply any redirects.

What is a redirect?

A redirect is a substitution of a URL segment. Redirects can either be local or absolute. Local redirects replace a single segment with a different one. Absolute redirects replace the whole URL. Redirects are local unless you prefix the URL with a slash.

The provided configuration has only one redirect rule: { path: '', pathMatch: 'full', redirectTo: '/inbox' }, that is, replace / with /inbox. This redirect is absolute because the redirectTo value starts with a slash.

Since we are navigating to `/inbox/33/messages/44` and not `/`, the router will not apply any redirects, and the URL will stay as is.

Recognizing states

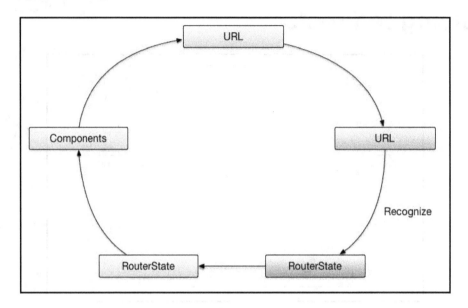

Next, the router will derive a router state from the URL. To understand how this phase works, we need to learn a bit about how the router matches the URL.

The router goes through the array of routes, one by one, checking if the URL starts with a route's path. Here it will check that `/inbox/33/messages/44` starts with `:folder`. It does, since `:folder` is what is called a **variable segment**. It is a parameter where normally you'd expect to find a constant string. Since it is a variable, virtually any string will match it. In our case `inbox` will match it. So the router will set the `folder` parameter to `inbox`, then it will take the children configuration items, the rest of the URL `33/messages/44`, and will carry on matching. As a result, the `id` parameter will be set to `33`, and, finally, the `messages/:id` route will be matched with the second `id` parameter set to `44`.

If the taken path through the configuration does not "consume" the whole URL, the router backtracks to try an alternative path. If it is impossible to match the whole URL, the navigation fails. But if it works, the router state representing the future state of the application will be constructed.

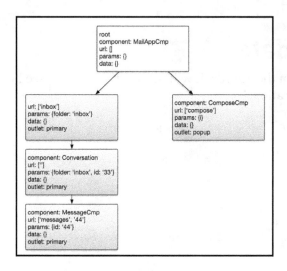

A router state consists of activated routes. And each activated route can be associated with a component. Also, note that we always have an activated route associated with the root component of the application.

Running guards

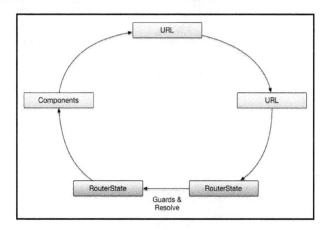

At this stage we have a future router state. Next, the router will check that transitioning to the new state is permitted. It will do this by running guards. We will cover guards in detail in next chapters. For now, it is sufficient to say that a guard is a function that the router runs to make sure that a navigation to a certain URL is permitted.

Resolving data

After the router has run the guards, it will resolve the data. To see how it works, let's tweak our preceding configuration:

```
[
  {
    path: ':folder',
    children: [
      {
        path: '',
        component: ConversationsCmp,
        resolve: {
          conversations: ConversationsResolver
        }
      }
    ]
  }
]
```

Where `ConversationsResolver` is defined as follows:

```
@Injectable()
class ConversationsResolver implements Resolve<any> {
  constructor(private repo: ConversationsRepo, private currentUser: User)
{}

  resolve(route: ActivatedRouteSnapshot, state: RouteStateSnapshot):
      Promise<Conversation[]> {
    return this.repo.fetchAll(route.params['folder'], this.currentUser);
  }
}
```

Finally, we need to register `ConversationsResolver` when bootstrapping our application:

```
@NgModule({
  //...
  providers: [ConversationsResolver],
  bootstrap: [MailAppCmp]
})
class MailModule {
}

platformBrowserDynamic().bootstrapModule(MailModule);
```

Now when navigating to /inbox, the router will create a router state, with an activated route for the conversations component. That route will have the folder parameter set to inbox. Using this parameter with the current user, we can fetch all the inbox conversations for that user.

We can access the resolved data by injecting the activated route object into the conversations component:

```
@Component({
  template: `
    <conversation *ngFor="let c of conversations | async"></conversation>
  `
})
class ConversationsCmp {
  conversations: Observable<Conversation[]>;
  constructor(route: ActivatedRoute) {
    this.conversations = route.data.pluck('conversations');
  }
}
```

Activating components

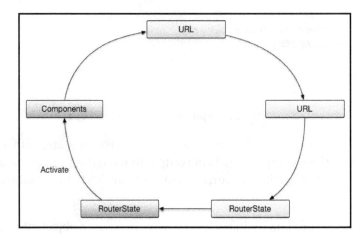

At this point, we have a router state. The router can now activate this state by instantiating all the needed components, and placing them into appropriate router outlets.

To understand how it works, let's take a look at how we use router outlets in a component template.

The root component of the application has two outlets: primary and popup.

```
@Component({
  template: `
    ...
    <router-outlet></router-outlet>

    ...
    <router-outlet name="popup"></router-outlet>
  `
})
class MailAppCmp {
}
```

Other components, such as ConversationCmp, have only one:

```
@Component({
  template: `
    ...
    <router-outlet></router-outlet>
    ...
  `
```

```
})
class ConversationCmp {
}
```

Other components, such as `ConversationCmp`, have only one:

```
@Component({
  template: `
    ...
    <router-outlet></router-outlet>
    ...
  `
})
class ConversationCmp {
}
```

Now imagine we are navigating to `/inbox/33/messages/44(popup:compose)`.

That's what the router will do. First, it will instantiate `ConversationCmp` and place it into the primary outlet of the root component. Then, it will place a new instance of `ComposeCmp` into the `'popup'` outlet. Finally, it will instantiate a new instance of `MessageCmp` and place it in the primary outlet of the just created conversation component.

Using parameters

Often components rely on parameters or resolved data. For instance, the conversation component probably need to access the conversation object. We can get the parameters and the data by injecting `ActivatedRoute`.

```
@Component({...})
class ConversationCmp {
  conversation: Observable<Conversation>;
  id: Observable<string>;

  constructor(r: ActivatedRoute) {
    // r.data is an observable
    this.conversation = r.data.map(d => d.conversation);

    // r.params is an observable
    this.id = r.params.map(p => p.id);
  }
}
```

If we navigate from
`inbox/33/messages/44(popup:compose)` to `/inbox/34/messages/45(popup:compo se)`, the data observable will emit a new `map` with the new object, and the conversation component will display the information about Conversation 34.

As you can see the router exposes parameters and data as observables, which is convenient most of the time, but not always. Sometimes what we want is a snapshot of the state that we can examine at once.

```
@Component({...})
class ConversationCmp {
  conversation: Conversation;
  constructor(r: ActivatedRoute) {
    const s: ActivatedRouteSnapshot = r.snapshot;
    this.conversation = s.data['conversation']; // Conversation
  }
}
```

Navigation

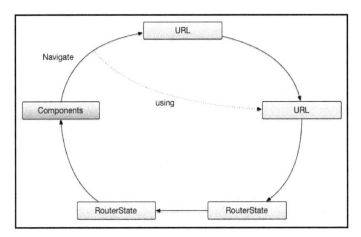

So at this point the router has created a router state and instantiated the components. Next, we need to be able to navigate from this router state to another one. There are two ways to accomplish this: imperatively, by calling `router.navigate`, or declaratively, by using the `routerLink` directive.

Imperative navigation

To navigate imperatively, inject the Router service and call `navigate`:

```
@Component({...})
class MessageCmp {
  public id: string;
  constructor(private route: ActivatedRoute, private router: Router) {
    route.params.subscribe(_ => this.id = _.id);
  }

  openPopup(e) {
    this.router.navigate([{outlets: {popup: ['message',
    this.id]}}]).then(_ => {
      // navigation is done
    });
  }
}
```

RouterLink

Another way to navigate around is by using the `routerLink` routerLink directive:

```
@Component({
  template: `
    <a [routerLink]="['/', {outlets: {popup: ['message',
    this.id]}}]">Edit</a>
  `
})
class MessageCmp {
  public id: string;
  constructor(private route: ActivatedRoute) {
    route.params.subscribe(_ => this.id = _.id);
  }
}
```

This directive will also update the `href` attribute when applied to an <a> link element, so it is SEO friendly and the right-click open-in-new-browser-tab behavior we expect from regular links will work.

Summary

Let's look at all the operations of the Angular router one more time:

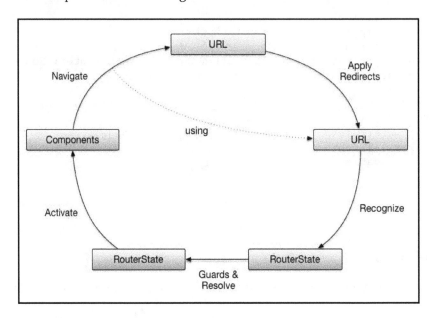

When the browser is loading `/inbox/33/messages/44(popup:compose)`, the router will do the following. First, it will apply redirects. In this example, none of them will be applied, and the URL will stay as is. Then the router will use this URL to construct a new router state:

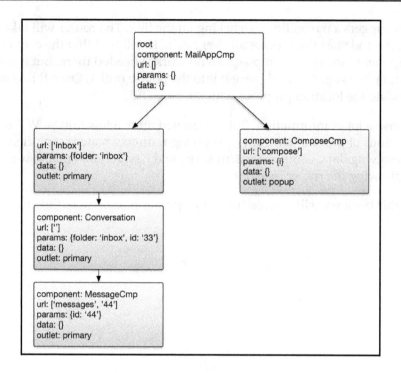

Next, the router will instantiate the conversation and message components:

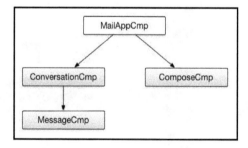

Now, let's say the message component has the following link in its template:

```
<a [routerLink]="[{outlets: {popup: ['message', this.id]}}]">Edit</a>
```

The router link directive will take the array and will set the `href` attribute to

`/inbox/33/messages/44(popup:message/44)`.

Now, the user triggers a navigation by clicking on the link. The router will take the constructed URL and start the process all over again: it will find that the conversation and message components are already in place. So no work is needed there. But it will create an instance of `PopupMessageCmp` and place it into the popup outlet. Once this is done, the router will update the location property with the new URL.

That was intense-a lot of information! But we learned quite a few things. We learned about the core operations of the Angular router: applying redirects, state recognition, running guards and resolving data, component activation, and navigation. Finally, we looked at an e2e example showing the router in action.

In the rest of this book we will discuss the same operations one more time in much greater depth.

3
URLs

When using the Angular router, a URL is just a serialized router state. Any state transition results in a URL change, and any URL change results in a state transition. Consequently, any link or navigation creates a URL.

Simple URL

Let's start with this simple URL /inbox/33.

This is how the router will encode the information about this URL:

```
const url: UrlSegment[] = [
  {path: 'inbox', params: {}},
  {path: '33', params: {}}
];
```

Where UrlSegment is defined as follows:

```
interface UrlSegment {
  path: string;
  params: {[name:string]:string};
}
```

We can use the ActivatedRoute object to get the URL segments consumed by the route:

```
class MessageCmp {
  constructor(r: ActivatedRoute) {
    r.url.forEach((u: UrlSegment[]) => {
      //...
    });
  }
}
```

Params

Let's soup it up a little by adding matrix or route-specific parameters, so the result URL looks like this: `/inbox;a=v1/33;b1=v1;b2=v2`:

```
[
  {path: 'inbox', params: {a: 'v1'}},
  {path: '33', params: {b1: 'v1', b2: 'v2'}}
]
```

Matrix parameters are scoped to a particular URL segment. Because of this, there is no risk of name collisions.

Query params

Sometimes, however, you want to share some parameters across many activated routes, and that's what query params are for. For instance, given this URL `/inbox/33?token=23756`, we can access `token` in any component:

```
class ConversationCmp {
  constructor(r: ActivateRoute) {
    r.queryParams.forEach((p) => {
      const token = p['token']
    });
  }
}
```

Since query parameters are not scoped, they should not be used to store route-specific information.

The fragment (for example, `/inbox/33#fragment`) is similar to query params:

```
class ConversationCmp {
  constructor(r: ActivatedRoute) {
    r.fragment.forEach((f:string) => {

    });
  }
}
```

Secondary segments

Since a router state is a tree, and the URL is nothing but a serialized state, the URL is a serialized tree. In all the examples so far every segment had only one child. For instance in /inbox/33 the 33 segment is a child of inbox, and inbox is a child of the / root segment. We called such children **primary**. Now look at this example:

```
/inbox/33(popup:message/44)
```

Here the root has two children **inbox** and **message**:

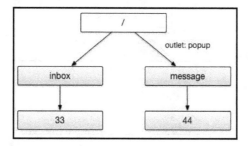

The router encodes multiple secondary children using a //.

```
/inbox/33(popup:message/44//help:overview)
```

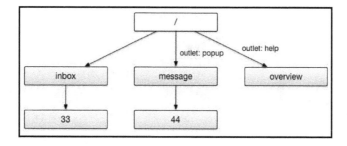

If some other segment, not the root, has multiple children, the router will encode it as follows:

```
/inbox/33/(messages/44//side:help)
```

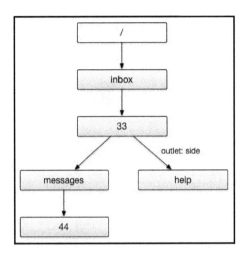

4

URL Matching

At the core of the Angular router lies a powerful URL matching engine, which transforms URLs and converts them into router states. Understanding how this engine works is important for implementing advanced use cases.

Once again, let's use this configuration:

```
[
  { path: '', pathMatch: 'full', redirectTo: '/inbox' },
  {
    path: ':folder',
    children: [
      {
        path: '',
        component: ConversationsCmp
      },
      {
        path: ':id',
        component: ConversationCmp,
        children: [
          { path: 'messages', component: MessagesCmp },
          { path: 'messages/:id', component: MessageCmp }
        ]
      }
    ]
  },
  {
    path: 'compose',
    component: ComposeCmp,
    outlet: 'popup'
  },
  {
    path: 'message/:id',
    component: PopupMessageCmp,
```

```
        outlet: 'popup'
    }
  ]
```

First, note that every route is defined by two key parts:

- How it matches the URL
- What it does once the URL is matched

It is important that the second concern, the action, does not affect the matching.

And let's say we are navigating to `/inbox/33/messages/44`.

This is how matching works:

The router goes through the provided array of routes, one by one, checking if the unconsumed part of the URL starts with a route's path.

Here it checks that `/inbox/33/messages/44` starts with `:folder`. It does. So the router sets the `folder` parameter to `inbox`, then it takes the children of the matched route, the rest of the URL, which is `33/messages/44`, and carries on matching.

The router will check that `33/messages/44` starts with `''`, and it does, since we interpret every string to begin with the empty string. Unfortunately, the route does not have any children and we haven't consumed the whole URL. So the router will backtrack to try the next route `path: ':id'`.

This one will work. The `id` parameter will be set to `33`, and finally the `messages/:id` route will be matched, and the second `id` parameter will be set to `44`.

Backtracking

Let's illustrate backtracking one more time. If the taken path through the configuration does not "consume" the whole url, the router backtracks to try an alternative path.

Say we have this configuration:

```
  [
    {
      path: 'a',
      children: [
        {
          path: 'b',
          component: ComponentB
```

```
      }
    ]
  },
  {
    path: ':folder',
    children: [
      {
        path: 'c',
        component: ComponentC
      }
    ]
  }
]
```

When navigating to /a/c, the router will start with the first route. The /a/c URL starts with path: 'a', so the router will try to match /c with b. Because it is unable to do that, it will backtrack and will match a with :folder, and then c with c.

Depth-first

The router doesn't try to find the best match, that is, it does not have any notion of specificity. It is satisfied with the first one that consumes the whole URL.

```
[
  {
    path: ':folder',
    children: [
      {
        path: 'b',
        component: ComponentB1
      }
    ]
  },
  {
    path: 'a',
    children: [
      {
        path: 'b',
        component: ComponentB2
      }
    ]
  }
]
```

When navigating to /a/b, the first route will be matched even though the second one appears to be **specific**.

Wildcards

We have seen that path expressions can contain two types of segments:

- constant segments (for example, path: 'messages')
- variable segments (for example, path: ':folder')

Using just these two we can handle most use cases. Sometimes, however, what we want is the "otherwise" route. The route that will match against any provided URL. That's what wildcard routes are. In the following example we have a wildcard route { path: '**', redirectTo: '/notfound' } that will match any URL that we were not able to match otherwise and will activate NotFoundCmp.

```
[
  {
    path: ':folder',
    children: [
      {
        path: '',
        component: ConversationsCmp
      },
      {
        path: ':id',
        component: ConversationCmp,
        children: [
          { path: 'messages', component: MessagesCmp },
          { path: 'messages/:id', component: MessageCmp }
        ]
      }
    ]
  }
  { path: '**', component: NotFoundCmp }
]
```

The wildcard route will "consume" all the URL segments, so NotFoundCmp can access those via the injected ActivatedRoute.

Empty-path routes

If you look at our configuration once again, you will see that some routes have the path set to an empty string. What does it mean?

```
[
  {
    path: ':folder',
    children: [
      {
        path: '',
        component: ConversationsCmp
      }
    ]
  }
]
```

By setting `path` to an empty string, we create a route that instantiates a component but does not "consume" any URL segments. This means that if we navigate to `/inbox`, the router will do the following:

First, it will check that `/inbox` starts with `:folder`, which it does. So it will take what is left of the URL, which is `''`, and the children of the route. Next, it will check that `''` starts with `''`, which it does! So the result of all this is the following router state:

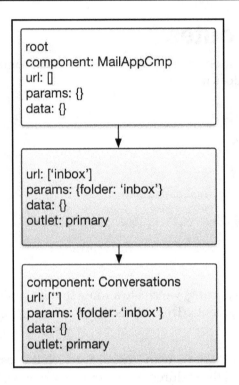

Empty path routes can have children, and, in general, behave like normal routes. The only special thing about them is that they inherit matrix parameters of their parents. This means that this URL /inbox;expand=true will result in the router state where two activated routes have the expand parameter set to true:

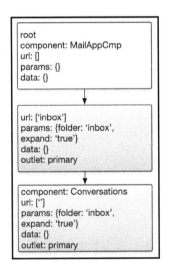

Matching strategies

By default the router checks if the URL starts with the path property of a route, that is, it checks if the URL is prefixed with the path. This is an implicit default, but we can set this strategy explicitly, as follows:

```
// identical to {path: 'a', component: ComponentA}

  {path : 'a' , pathMatch:'prefix',component: ComponentA}
```

The router supports a second matching strategy-full, which checks that the path is "equal" to what is left in the URL. This is mostly important for redirects. To see why, let's look at this example:

```
[
  { path: '', redirectTo: '/inbox' },
  {
    path: ':folder',
    children: [
      ...
    ]
  }
]
```

Because the default matching strategy is prefix, and any URL starts with an empty string, the router will always match the first route. Even if we navigate to /inbox, the router will apply the first redirect. Our intent, however, is to match the second route when navigating to /inbox, and redirect to /inbox when navigating to /. Now, if we change the matching strategy to full, the router will apply the redirect only when navigating to /.

Componentless routes

Most of the routes in the configuration have either the redirectTo or component properties set, but some have neither. For instance, look at path: ':folder' route in the following configuration:

```
{
  path: ':folder',
  children: [
    {
      path: '',
      component: ConversationsCmp
    },
    {
```

```
      path: ':id',
      component: ConversationCmp,
      children: [
        { path: 'messages', component: MessagesCmp },
        { path: 'messages/:id', component: MessageCmp }
      ]
    }
  ]
}
```

We called such routes componentless routes. Their main purpose is to consume URL segments, provide some data to its children, and do it without instantiating any components.

The parameters captured by a componentless route will be merged into their children's parameters. The data resolved by a componentless route will be merged as well. In this example, both the child routes will have the folder parameter in their parameters maps.

This particular example could have been easily rewritten as follows:

```
[
  {
    path: ':folder',
    component: ConversationsCmp
  },
  {
    path: ':folder/:id',
    component: ConversationCmp,
    children: [
      { path: 'messages', component: MessagesCmp },
      { path: 'messages/:id', component: MessageCmp }
    ]
  }
]
```

We have to duplicate the `:folder` parameter, but overall it works. Sometimes, however, there is no other good option but to use a componentless route.

Sibling components using same data

For instance, it is useful to share parameters between sibling components.

In the following example we have two components-`MessageListCmp` and `MessageDetailsCmp`-that we want to put next to each other, and both of them require the message id parameter. The `MessageListCmp` component uses the id to highlight the selected message, and `MessageDetailsCmp` uses it to show the information about the message.

One way to model that would be to create a bogus parent component, which both `MessageListCmp` and `MessageDetailsCmp` can get the id parameter from, that is, we can model this solution with the following configuration:

```
[
  {
    path: 'messages/:id',
    component: MessagesParentCmp,
    children: [
      {
        path: '',
        component: MessageListCmp
      },
      {
        path: '',
```

```
            component: MessageDetailsCmp,
            outlet: 'details'
        }
      ]
    }
  ]
```

With this configuration in place, navigating to /messages/11 will result in this component tree:

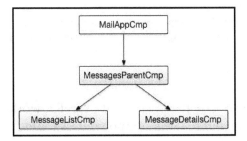

This solution has a problem-we need to create the bogus component, which serves no real purpose. That's where componentless routes are a good solution:

```
[
  {
    path: 'messages/:id',
    children: [
      {
        path: '',
        component: MessageListCmp
      },
      {
        path: '',
        component: MessageDetailsCmp,
        outlet: 'details'
      }
    ]
  }
]
```

Now, when navigating to `/messages/11`, the router will create the following component tree:

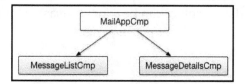

Composing componentless and empty-path routes

What is really exciting about all these features is that they compose very nicely. So we can use them together to handle advanced use cases in just a few lines of code.

Let me give you an example. We have learned that we can use empty-path routes to instantiate components without consuming any URL segments, and we can use componentless routes to consume URL segments without instantiating components. What about combining them?

```
[
  {
    path: '',
    canActivate: [CanActivateMessagesAndContacts],
    resolve: {
      token: TokenNeededForBothMessagsAndContacts
    },

    children: [
      {
        path: 'messages',
        component: MesssagesCmp
      },
      {
        path: 'contacts',
        component: ContactsCmp
      }
    ]
  }
]
```

Here we have defined a route that neither consumes any URL segments nor creates any components, but used merely for running guards and fetching data that will be used by both `MesssagesCmp` and `ContactsCmp`. Duplicating these in the children is not an option as both the guard and the data resolver can be expensive asynchronous operations and we want to run them only once.

Summary

We've learned a lot! First, we talked about how the router does matching. It goes through the provided routes, one by one, checking if the URL starts with a route's path. Then, we learned that the router does not have any notion of specificity. It just traverses the configuration in the depth-first order, and it stops after finding the path matching the whole URL, that is, the order of routes in the configuration matters. After that, we talked about empty-path routes that do not consume any URL segments, and about componentless routes that do not instantiate any components. We showed how we can use them to handle advanced use cases.

5
Redirects

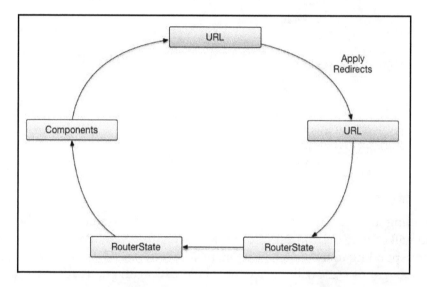

Using redirects we can transform the URL before the router creates a router state out of it. This is useful for normalizing URLs and large scale refactorings.

Local and absolute redirects

Redirects can be local and absolute. Local redirects replace a single URL segment with a different one. Absolute redirects replace the whole URL.

If the `redirectTo` value starts with a /, then it is an absolute redirect. The next example shows the difference between relative and absolute redirects.

```
[
  {
    path: ':folder/:id',
    component: ConversationCmp,
    children: [
      {
        path: 'contacts/:name',
        redirectTo: '/contacts/:name'
      },
      {
        path: 'legacy/messages/:id',
        redirectTo: 'messages/:id'
      },
      {
        path: 'messages/:id',
        component: MessageCmp
      }
    ]
  },
  {
    path: 'contacts/:name',
    component: ContactCmp
  }
]
```

When navigating to `/inbox/33/legacy/messages/44`, the router will apply the second redirect and will change the URL to `/inbox/33/messages/44`. In other words, the part of the URL corresponding to the matched segment will be replaced. But navigating to `/inbox/33/contacts/jim` will replace the whole URL with `/contacts/jim`.

Note that a `redirectTo` value can contain variable segments captured by the path expression (for example, `:name`, `:id`). All the matrix parameters of the corresponding segments matched by the path expression will be preserved as well.

One redirect at a time

You can set up redirects at different levels of your router configuration. Let's modify the preceding example to illustrate this:

```
[
  {
    path: 'legacy/:folder/:id',
    redirectTo: ':folder/:id'
  },
  {
    path: ':folder/:id',
    component: ConversationCmp,
    children: [
      {
        path: 'legacy/messages/:id',
        redirectTo: 'messages/:id'
      },
      {
        path: 'messages/:id',
        component: MessageCmp
      }
    ]
  }
]
```

When navigating to /legacy/inbox/33/legacy/messages/44, the router will first apply the outer redirect, transforming the URL to /inbox/33/legacy/messages/44. After that the router will start processing the children of the second route and will apply the inner redirect, resulting in this URL: /inbox/33/messages/44.

One constraint the router imposes is at any level of the configuration the router applies only one redirect, that is, redirects cannot be chained.

For instance, say we have this configuration:

```
[
  {
    path: 'legacy/messages/:id',
    redirectTo: 'messages/:id'
  },
  {
    path: 'messages/:id',
    redirectTo: 'new/messages/:id'
  },
  {
    path: 'new/messages/:id',
```

```
        component: MessageCmp
    }
  ]
```

When navigating to `legacy/messages/:id`, the router will replace the URL with `messages/:id` and will stop there. It won't redirect to `new/messages/:id`. A similar constraint is applied to absolute redirects: once an absolute redirect is matched, the redirect phase stops.

Using redirects to normalize URLs

We often use redirects for URL normalization. Say we want both `mail-app.vsavkin.com` and `mail-app.vsavkin.com/inbox` render the same UI. We can use a redirect to achieve that:

```
[
  { path: '', pathMatch: 'full', redirectTo: '/inbox' },
  {
    path: ':folder',
    children: [
      ...
    ]
  }
]
```

We can also use redirects to implement a not-found page:

```
[
  {
    path: ':folder',
    children: [
      {
        path: '',
        component: ConversationsCmp
      },
      {
        path: ':id',
        component: ConversationCmp,
        children: [
          { path: 'messages', component: MessagesCmp },
          { path: 'messages/:id', component: MessageCmp }
        ]
      }
      { path: '**', redirectTo: '/notfound/conversation' }
```

```
    ]
  }
  { path: 'notfound/:objectType', component: NotFoundCmp }
]
```

Using redirects to enable refactoring

Another big use case for using redirects is to enable large scale refactorings. Such refactorings can take months to complete, and, consequently, we will not be able to update all the URLs in the whole application in one go. We will need to do in phases. By using redirects we can keep the old URLs working while migrating to the new implementation.

6
Router State

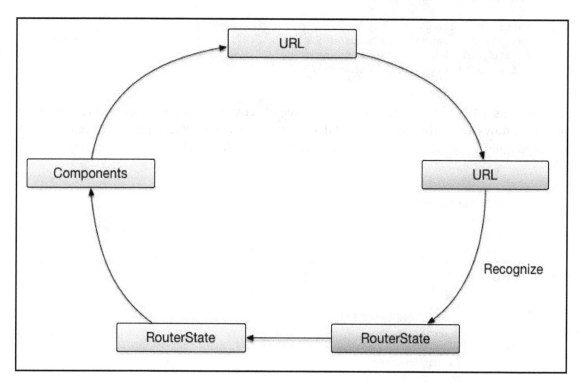

During a navigation, after redirects have been applied, the router creates a
`RouterStateSnapshot`.

What is RouterStateSnapshot?

```
interface RouterStateSnapshot {
  root: ActivatedRouteSnapshot;
}

interface ActivatedRouteSnapshot {
  url: UrlSegment[];
  params: {[name:string]:string};
  data: {[name:string]:any};

  queryParams: {[name:string]:string};
  fragment: string;

  root: ActivatedRouteSnapshot;
  parent: ActivatedRouteSnapshot;
  firstchild: ActivatedRouteSnapshot;
  children: ActivatedRouteSnapshot[];
}
```

As you can see `RouterStateSnapshot` is a tree of activated route snapshots. Every node in this tree knows about the "consumed" URL segments, the extracted parameters, and the resolved data. To make it clearer, let's look at this example:

```
[
  {
    path: ':folder',
    children: [
      {
        path: '',
        component: ConversationsCmp
      },
      {
        path: ':id',
        component: ConversationCmp,
        children: [
          {
            path: 'messages',
            component: MessagesCmp
          },
          {
            path: 'messages/:id',
            component: MessageCmp,
            resolve: {
              message: MessageResolver
            }
          }
```

```
      ]
    }
  ]
}
]
```

When we are navigating to `/inbox/33/messages/44`, the router will look at the URL and will construct the following `RouterStateSnapshot`:

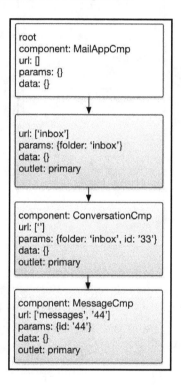

After that the router will instantiate `ConversationCmp` with `MessageCmp` in it.

Now imagine we are navigating to a different URL: `/inbox/33/messages/45`, which will result in the following snapshot:

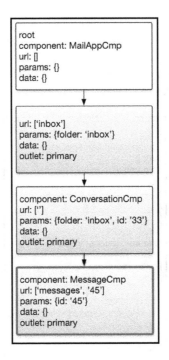

To avoid unnecessary DOM modifications, the router will reuse the components when the parameters of the corresponding routes change. In this example, the `id` parameter of the message component has changed from `44` to `45`. This means that we cannot just inject an `ActivatedRouteSnapshot` into `MessageCmp` because the snapshot will always have the `id` parameter set to `44`, that is, it will get stale.

The router state snapshot represents the state of the application at a moment in time, hence the name `snapshot`. But components can stay active for hours, and the data they show can change. So having only snapshots won't cut it-we need a data structure that allows us to deal with changes.

Introducing RouterState!

```
interface RouterState {
  snapshot: RouterStateSnapshot; //returns current snapshot

  root: ActivatedRoute;
}

interface ActivatedRoute {
  snapshot: ActivatedRouteSnapshot; //returns current snapshot

  url: Observable<UrlSegment[]>;
  params: Observable<{[name:string]:string}>;
  data: Observable<{[name:string]:any}>;

  queryParams: Observable<{[name:string]:string}>;
  fragment: Observable<string>;

  root: ActivatedRout;
  parent: ActivatedRout;
  firstchild: ActivatedRout;
  children: ActivatedRout[];
}
```

The `RouterState` and `ActivatedRoute` interface are similar to their snapshot counterparts except that they expose all the values as observables, which are great for dealing with values changing over time.

Any component instantiated by the router can inject its `ActivatedRoute`.

```
@Component({
  template: `
      Title: {{(message|async).title}}
      ...
  `
})
class MessageCmp {
  message: Observable<Message>;
  constructor(r: ActivatedRoute) {
    this.message = r.data.map(d => d.message);
  }
}
```

If we navigate from `/inbox/33/messages/44` to `/inbox/33/messages/45`, the data observable will emit a new set of data with the new message object, and the component will display Message 45.

Accessing snapshots

The router exposes parameters and data as observables, which is convenient most of the time, but not always. Sometimes what we want is a snapshot of the state that we can examine at once.

```
@Component({...})
class MessageCmp {
  constructor(r: ActivatedRoute) {
    r.url.subscribe(() => {
      r.snapshot; // any time url changes, this callback is fired
    });
  }
}
```

ActivatedRoute

The `ActivatedRoute` interface provides access to the url, params, data, queryParams, and fragment observables. We will look at each of them in detail, but first let's examine the relationships between them.

URL changes are the source of any changes in a route. And it has to be this way as the user has the ability to modify the location directly.

Any time the URL changes, the router derives a new set of parameters from it: the router takes the positional parameters (for example, `:id`) of the matched URL segments and the matrix parameters of the last matched URL segment and combines those. This operation is pure: the URL has to change for the parameters to change. Or in other words, the same URL will always result in the same set of parameters.

Next, the router invokes the route's data resolvers and combines the result with the provided static data. Since data resolvers are arbitrary functions, the router cannot guarantee that you will get the same object when given the same URL. Even more, often this cannot be the case! The URL contains the id of a resource, which is fixed, and data resolvers fetch the content of that resource, which often varies over time.

Finally, the activated route provides the `queryParams` and fragment observables. In opposite to other observables, that are scoped to a particular route, query parameters and fragment are shared across multiple routes.

URL

Given the following:

```
@Component({...})
class ConversationCmp- {
  constructor(r: ActivatedRoute) {
    r.url.subscribe((s:UrlSegment[]) => {
      console.log("url", s);
    });
  }
}
```

And navigating first to `/inbox/33/messages/44` and then to `/inbox/33/messages/45`, we will see:

```
url [{path: 'messages', params: {}}, {path: '44', params: {}}]
url [{path: 'messages', params: {}}, {path: '45', params: {}}]
```

We do not often listen to URL changes as those are too low level. One use case where it can be practical is when a component is activated by a wildcard route. Since in this case the array of URL segments is not fixed, it might be useful to examine it to show different data to the user.

Params

Given the following:

```
@Component({...})
class MessageCmp {
  constructor(r: ActivatedRoute) {
    r.params.subscribe((p => {
      console.log("params", params);
    });
  }
}
```

And when navigating first to `/inbox/33/messages;a=1/44;b=1` and then to `/inbox/33/messages;a=2/45;b=2`, we will see

```
params {id: '44', b: '1'}
params {id: '45', b: '2'}
```

First thing to note is that the `id` parameter is a string (when dealing with URLs we always work with strings). Second, the route gets only the matrix parameters of its last URL segment. That is why the `a` parameter is not present.

Data

Let's tweak the preceding configuration to see how the data observable works:

```
{
  path: 'messages/:id',
  component: MessageCmp,
  data: {
    allowReplyAll: true
  },
  resolve: {
    message: MessageResolver
  }
}
```

Where `MessageResolver` is defined as follows:

```
class MessageResolver implements Resolve<any> {
  constructor(private repo: ConversationsRepo, private currentUser: User)
{}

  resolve(route: ActivatedRouteSnapshot, state: RouteStateSnapshot):
    Promise<Message> {
    return this.repo.fetchMessage(route.params['id'],
    this.currentUser);
  }
}
```

The `data` property is used for passing a fixed object to an activated route. It does not change throughout the lifetime of the application. The `resolve` property is used for dynamic data.

Note that in the preceding configuration the line `message: MessageResolver` does not tell the router to instantiate the resolver. It instructs the router to fetch one using dependency injection. This means that you have to register `MessageResolver` in the list of providers somewhere. Once the router has fetched the resolver, it will call the `resolve` method on it. The method can return a promise, an observable, or any other object. If the return value is a promise or an observable, the router will wait for that promise or observable to complete before proceeding with the activation.

The resolver does not have to be a class implementing the Resolve interface. It can also be a function:

```
function resolver(route: ActivatedRouteSnapshot, state:
RouteStateSnapshot):
  Promise<Message> {
  return repo.fetchMessage(route.params['id'], this.currentUser);
}
```

The router combines the resolved and static data into a single property, which you can access, as follows:

```
@Component({...})
class MessageCmp {
  constructor(r: ActivatedRoute) {
    r.data.subscribe((d => {
      console.log('data', d);
    });
  }
}
```

When navigating first to `/inbox/33/message/44` and then to `/inbox/33/messages/45`, we will see

```
data {allowReplyAll: true, message: {id: 44, title: 'Rx Rocks', ...}}
data {allowReplyAll: true, message: {id: 45, title: 'Angular Rocks',
...}}
```

Query params and fragment

In opposite to other observables, that are scoped to a particular route, query parameters and fragment are shared across multiple routes.

```
@Component({...})
class MessageCmp {
  debug: Observable <string>;
  fragment: Observable <string>;

  constructor(route: ActivatedRoute) {
    this.debug = route.queryParams.map(p => p.debug);
    this.fragment = route.fragment;
  }
}
```

7
Links and Navigation

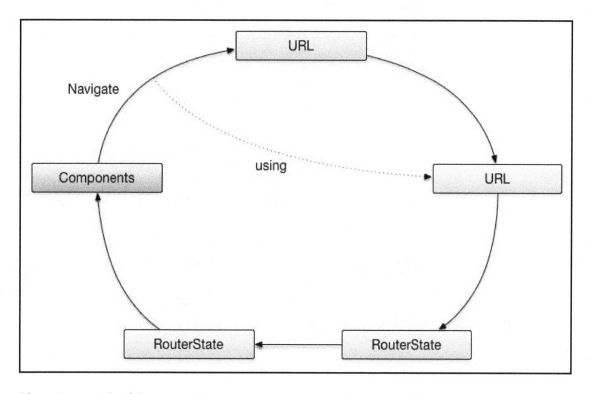

The primary job of the router is to manage navigation between different router states. There are two ways to accomplish this: imperatively, by calling `router.navigate`, or declaratively, by using the RouterLink directive.

As before, let's assume the following configuration:

```
[
  { path: '', pathMatch: 'full', redirectTo: '/inbox' },
  {
    path: ':folder',
    children: [
      {
        path: '',
        component: ConversationsCmp
      },
      {
        path: ':id',
        component: ConversationCmp,
        children: [
          { path: 'messages', component: MessagesCmp },
          { path: 'messages/:id', component: MessageCmp }
        ]
      }
    ]
  },
  {
    path: 'compose',
    component: ComposeCmp,
    outlet: 'popup'
  },
  {
    path: 'message/:id',
    component: PopupMessageCmp,
    outlet: 'popup'
  }
]
```

Imperative navigation

To navigate imperatively, inject the Router service and call `navigate` or `navigateByUrl` on it. Why two methods and not one?

Using `router.navigateByUrl` is similar to changing the location bar directly–we are providing the "whole" new URL. Whereas `router.navigate` creates a new URL by applying a series of passed-in commands, a patch, to the current URL.

To see the difference clearly, imagine that the current URL is `/inbox/11/messages/22(popup:compose)`.

With this URL, calling `router.navigateByUrl('/inbox/33/messages/44')` will result in `/inbox/33/messages/44`, and calling `router.navigate('/inbox/33/messages/44')` will result in `/inbox/33/messages/44(popup:compose)`.

Router.navigate

Let's see what we can do with `router.navigate`.

Passing an array or a string

Passing a string is sugar for passing an array with a single element.

```
router.navigate('/inbox/33/messages/44')
```

is sugar for

```
router.navigate (['/inbox/33/messages/44'])
```

which itself is sugar for

```
router.navigate (['/inbox', 33, 'messages', 44])
```

Passing matrix params

```
router.navigate([
  '/inbox', 33, {details: true}, 'messages', 44, {mode: 'preview'}
])
```

navigates to

```
'/inbox/33;details=true/messages/44;mode=preview(popup:compose)'
```

Updating secondary segments

```
router.navigate([{outlets: {popup: 'message/22'])
```

navigates to

```
'/inbox/11/messages/22(popup:message/22)'
```

We can also update multiple segments at once, as follows:

```
router.navigate([
  {outlets: {primary: 'inbox/33/messages/44', popup: 'message/44'}}
])
```

navigates to

```
'/inbox/33/messages/44(popup:message/44)'
```

And, of course, this works for any segment, not just the root one.

```
router.navigate([
  '/inbox/33', {outlets: {primary: 'messages/44', help: 'message/123'}}
])
```

navigates to

```
'/inbox/33/(messages/44//help:messages/123)(popup:message/44)'
```

We can also remove segments by setting them to `null`.

```
router.navigate([{outlets: {popup: null])
```

navigates to

```
'/inbox/11/messages/22'
```

Relative navigation

By default, the `navigate` method applies the provided commands starting from the root URL segment, that is, the navigation is absolute. We can make it relative by providing the starting route, like this:

```
@Component({...})
class MessageCmp {
  constructor(private route: ActivatedRoute, private router: Router) {}

  goToConversation() {
    this.router.navigate('../../', {relativeTo: this.route});
  }
}
```

Let's look at a few examples, given we are providing the `path: 'message/:id'` route.

```
router.navigate('details', {relativeTo: this.route})
```

navigates to

```
'/inbox/33/messages/44/details(popup:compose)'
```

The `../` allows us to skip one URL segment.

```
router.navigate('../55', {relativeTo: this.route})
```

navigates to

```
'/inbox/33/messages/55(popup:compose)'
router.navigate('../../', {relativeTo: this.route})
```

navigates to

```
'/inbox/33(popup:compose)'
```

Forcing absolute navigation

If the first command starts with a slash, the navigation is absolute regardless if we provide a route or not.

Navigation is URL-based

Using `../` does not skip a route, but skips a URL segment. More generally, the router configuration has no affect on URL-generation. The router only looks at the current URL and the provided commands to generate a new URL.

Passing query params and fragment

By default the router resets query params during navigation. If this is the current URL:

```
'/inbox/11/messages/22?debug=true#section2'
```

Then calling

```
router.navigate('/inbox/33/message/44')
```

will navigate to

```
'/inbox/33/messages/44'
```

If we want to preserve the current query params and fragment, we can do the following:

```
router.navigate('/inbox/33/message/44',
  {preserveQueryParams: true, preserveFragment: true})
```

Or we always can provide new params and fragment, like this:

```
router.navigate('/inbox/33/message/44',
  {queryParams: {debug: false}, fragment: 'section3'})
```

RouterLink

Another way to navigate around is by using the RouterLink directive:

```
@Component({
  template: `
    <a [routerLink]="/inbox/33/messages/44">Open Message 44</a>
  `
})
class SomeComponent {}
```

Behind the scenes RouterLink just calls `router.navigate` with the provided commands. If we do not start the first command with a slash, the navigation is relative to the route of the component.

Everything that we can pass to `router.navigate`, we can pass to `routerLink`. For instance:

```
<a [routerLink]="[{outlets: {primary: 'inbox/33/messages/44', popup:
'message/44'}}]">
  Open Message 44
</a>
```

As with `router.navigate`, we can set or preserve query params and fragment.

```
<a [routerLink]="/inbox/33/messages/44" preserveQueryParams
preserveFragment>
  Open Message 44
</a>

<a [routerLink]="/inbox/33/messages/44"
  [queryParams]="{debug:false}" [fragment]="section3">
  Open Message 44
</a>
```

This directive will also update the `href` attribute when applied to an `<a>` link element, so it is SEO friendly and the right-click open-in-new-browser-tab behavior we expect from regular links will work.

Active links

By using the RouterLinkActive directive, we can add a CSS class to an element when the link's route becomes active.

```
<a [routerLink]="/inbox" routerLinkActive="active-link">Inbox</a>
```

When the URL is either `/inbox` or `/inbox/33`, the `active-link` class will be added to the a tag. If the url changes, the class will be removed.

We can set more than one class, as follows:

```
<a [routerLink]="/inbox" routerLinkActive="class1 class2">Inbox</a>
```

```
<a [routerLink]="/inbox" routerLinkActive="['class1', 'class2']">Inbox</a>
```

Exact matching

We can make the matching exact by passing `"{exact: true}"`. This will add the classes only when the URL matches the link exactly. For instance, in the following example the `'active-link'` class will be added only when the URL is `'/inbox'`, not `'/inbox/33'`.

```
<a [routerLink]="/inbox" routerLinkActive="active-link"
   [routerLinkActiveOptions]="{exact: true}">
   Inbox
 </a>
```

Adding classes to ancestors

Finally, we can apply this directive to an ancestor of a RouterLink:

```
<div routerLinkActive="active-link" [routerLinkActiveOptions]="{exact:
true}">
  <a [routerLink]="/inbox">Inbox</a>
  <a [routerLink]="/drafts">Drafts</a>
</div>
```

This will set the `active-link` class on the `div` tag if the URL is either `/inbox` or `/drafts`.

Summary

That's a lot of information! So let's recap.

First, we established that the primary job of the router is to manage navigation. And there are two ways to do it: imperatively, by calling `router.navigate`, or declaratively, by using the RouterLink directive. We learned about the difference between `router.navigateByUrl` and `router.navigate`: one takes the whole URL, and the other one takes a patch it applies to the current URL. Then we talked about absolute and relative navigation. Finally, we saw how to use `[routerLink]` and `[routerLinkActive]` to set up navigation in the template.

8
Lazy Loading

Angular is built with the focus on mobile. That's why we put a lot of effort into making compiled and bundled Angular applications small. One of the techniques we use extensively is dead code elimination, which helped drop the size of a hello world application to only 20K. This is half the size of an analogous Angular application-an impressive result!

At some point, however, our application will be big enough, that even with this technique, the application file will be too large to be loaded at once. That's where lazy loading comes into play.

Lazy loading speeds up our application load time by splitting it into multiple bundles, and loading them on demand. We designed the router to make lazy loading simple and easy.

Example

We are going to continue using the mail app example, but this time we will add a new section, contacts, to our application. At launch, our application displays messages. Click the contacts button and it shows the contacts.

Let's start by sketching out our application:

```
main.ts:
import {Component, NgModule} from '@angular/core';
import {RouterModule} from '@angular/router';
import {platformBrowserDynamic} from '@angular/platform-browser-dynamic';

@Component({...}) class MailAppCmp {}
@Component({...}) class ConversationsCmp {}
@Component({...}) class ConversationCmp {}
```

```
@Component({...}) class ContactsCmp {}
@Component({...}) class ContactCmp {}

const ROUTES = [
  {
    path: 'contacts',
    children: [
      { path: '', component: ContactsCmp },
      { path: ':id', component: ContactCmp }
    ]
  },
  {
    path: ':folder',
    children: [
      { path: '', component: ConversationsCmp },
      { path: ':id', component: ConversationCmp, children: [...]}
    ]
  }
];


@NgModule({
  //...
  bootstrap: [MailAppCmp],
  imports: [RouterModule.forRoot(ROUTES)]
})
class MailModule {}

platformBrowserDynamic().bootstrapModule(MailModule);
```

The button showing the contacts UI can look like this:

```
<button [routerLink]="/contacts">Contacts</button>
```

In addition, we can also support linking to individual contacts, as follows:

```
<a [routerLink]="['/contacts', id]">Show Contact</a>
```

In the preceding code sample all the routes and components are defined together, in the same file. This is done for the simplicity sake. How the components are arranged does not really matter, as long as after the compilation we will have a single bundle file main.bundle.js, which will contain the whole application:

```
                    ┌─────────────────────────────┐
                    │   ┌─────────────────────┐   │
                    │   │    main.bundle.js    │   │
                    │   │                     │   │
                    │   │     MailAppCmp       │   │
                    │   │   ConversationsCmp   │   │
                    │   │   ConversationCmp    │   │
                    │   │     ContactsCmp      │   │
                    │   │      ContactCmp      │   │
                    │   └─────────────────────┘   │
                    └─────────────────────────────┘
```

Just one problem

There is one problem with this setup: even though `ContactsCmp` and `ContactCmp` are not displayed on load, they are still bundled up with the main part of the application. As a result, the initial bundle is larger than it could have been.

Two extra components may not seem like a big deal, but in a real application the contacts module can include dozens or even hundreds of components, together with all the services and helper functions they need.

A better setup would be to extract the contacts-related code into a separate module and load it on-demand. Let's see how we can do that.

Lazy loading

We start with extracting all the contacts-related components and routes into a separate file:

```
contacts.ts:
import {NgModule, Component} from '@angular/core';
import {RouterModule} from '@angular/router';

@Component({...}) class ContactsComponent {}
@Component({...}) class ContactComponent {}

const ROUTES = [
  { path: '', component: ContactsComponent },
  { path: ':id', component: ContactComponent }
];

@NgModule({
  imports: [RouterModule.forChild(ROUTES)]
```

```
})
class ContactsModule {}
```

In Angular an `ng` module is part of an application that can be bundled and loaded independently. So we have defined one in the preceding code.

Referring to lazily-loaded module

Now, after extracting the contacts module, we need to update the main module to refer to the newly extracted one:

```
const ROUTES = [
  {
    path: 'contacts',
    loadChildren: 'contacts.bundle.js',
  },
  {
    path: ':folder',
    children: [
      {
        path: '',
        component: ConversationsCmp
      },
      {
        path: ':id',
        component: ConversationCmp,
        children: [...]
      }
    ]
  }
];

@NgModule({
  //...
  bootstrap: [MailAppCmp],
  imports: [RouterModule.forRoot(ROUTES)]
})
class MailModule {}

platformBrowserDynamic().bootstrapModule(MailModule);
```

The `loadChildren` properly tells the router to fetch the `contacts.bundle.js` when and only when the user navigates to `contacts`, then merge the two router configurations, and, finally, activate the needed components.

By doing so we split the single bundle into two:

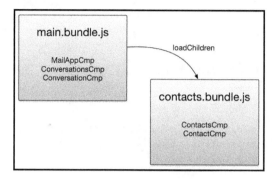

The bootstrap loads just the main bundle. The router won't load the contacts bundle until it is needed:

```
<button [routerLink]="/contacts">Contacts</button>

<a [routerLink]="['/contacts', id]">Show Contact</a>
```

Note that apart from the router configuration we don't have to change anything in the application after splitting it into multiple bundles: existing links and navigations are unchanged.

Deep linking

But it gets better! The router also supports deep linking into lazily-loaded modules.

To see what I mean imagine that the contacts module lazy loads another one:

```
contacts.ts:
import {Component, NgModule} from '@angular/core';
import {RouterModule} from '@angular/router';

@Component({...}) class AllContactsComponent {}
@Component({...}) class ContactComponent {}

const ROUTES = [
  { path: '', component: ContactsComponent },
  { path: ':id', component: ContactComponent, loadChildren:
'details.bundle.js' }
];

@NgModule({
```

```
    imports: [RouterModule.forChild(ROUTES)]
})
class ContactsModule {}

details.ts:

@Component({...}) class BriefComponent {}
@Component({...}) class DetailComponent {}

const ROUTES = [
  { path: '', component: BriefDetailComponent },
  { path: 'detail', component: DetailComponent },
];

@NgModule({
  imports: [RouterModule.forChild(ROUTES)]
})
class DetailModule {}
```

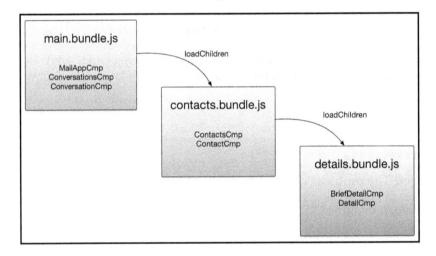

Imagine we have the following link in the main section or our application:

```
<a [routerLink]="['/contacts', id, 'detail', {full: true}]">
  Show Contact Detail
</a>
```

When clicking on the link, the router will first fetch the contacts module, then the details module. After that it will merge all the configurations and instantiate the needed components. Once again, from the link's perspective it makes no difference how we bundle our application. It just works.

Sync link generation

The RouterLink directive does more than handle clicks. It also sets the `<a>` tag's href attribute, so the user can right-click and "Open link in a new tab".

For instance, the preceding above will set the anchor's href attribute to `/contacts/13/detail;full=true`. And it will do it synchronously, without loading the configurations from the contacts or details bundles. Only when the user actually clicks on the link, the router will load all the needed configurations to perform the navigation.

Navigation is URL-based

Deep linking into lazily-loaded modules and synchronous link generation are possible only because the router's navigation is URL-based. Because the router does not have the notion of route names, it does not have to use any configuration to generate links. What we pass to `routerLink` (for example, `['/contacts', id, 'detail', {full: true}]`) is just an array of URL segments. In other words, link generation is purely mechanical and application independent.

This is an important design decision we have made early on because we knew that lazy loading is a key use case for using the router.

Customizing module loader

The built-in application module loader uses `SystemJS`. But we can provide our own implementation of the loader as follows:

```
@NgModule({
  //...
  bootstrap: [MailAppCmp],
  imports: [RouterModule.forRoot(ROUTES)],
  providers: [{provide: NgModuleFactoryLoader, useClass: MyCustomLoader}]
})
class MailModule {}

platformBrowserDynamic().bootstrapModule(MailModule);
```

You can look at `SystemJsNgModuleLoader` to see an example of a module loader.

Finally, you don't have to use the loader at all. Instead, you can provide a callback the route will use to fetch the module.

```
{
  path: 'contacts',
  loadChildren: () => System.import('somePath'),
}
```

Preloading modules

Lazy loading speeds up our application load time by splitting it into multiple bundles, and loading them on demand. We designed the router to make lazy loading transparent, so you can opt in and opt out of lazy loading with ease.

The issue with lazy loading, of course, is that when the user navigates to the lazy-loadable section of the application, the router will have to fetch the required modules from the server, which can take time.

To fix this problem we have added support for preloading. Now the router can preload lazy-loadable modules in the background while the user is interacting with our application.

This is how it works.

First, we load the initial bundle, which contains only the components we need to have to bootstrap our application. So it is as fast as it can be.

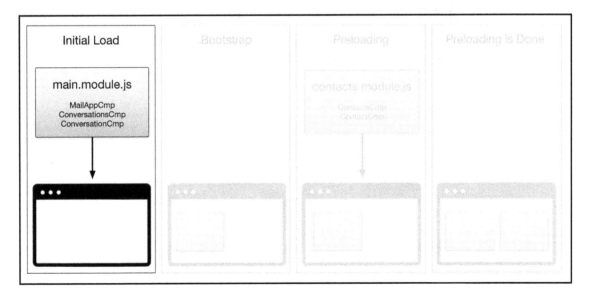

Then, we bootstrap the application using this small bundle.

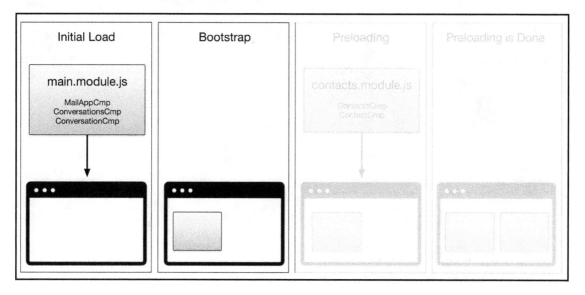

At this point the application is running, so the user can start interacting with it. While she is doing it, we, in the background, preload other modules.

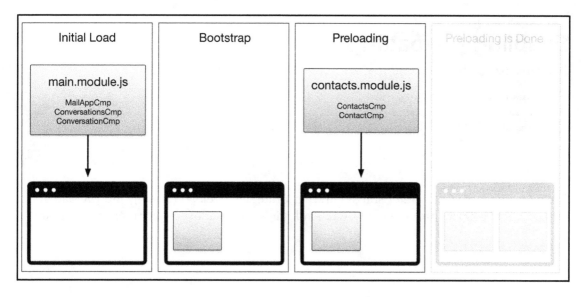

Finally, when she clicks on a link going to a lazy-loadable module, the navigation is instant.

We got the best of both worlds: the initial load time is as small as it can be, and subsequent navigations are instant.

Enabling preloading

To enable preloading we need to pass a preloading strategy into `forRoot`.

```
@NgModule({
  bootstrap: [MailAppCmp],
  imports: [RouterModule.forRoot(ROUTES,
    {preloadingStrategy: PreloadAllModules})]
})
class MailModule {}
```

The latest version of the router ships with two strategies: preload nothing and preload all modules, but you can provide your own. And it is actually a lot simpler than it may seem.

Custom preloading strategy

Say we don't want to preload all the modules. Rather, we would like to say explicitly, in the router configuration, what should be preloaded:

```
[
  {
    path: 'moduleA',
    loadChildren: './moduleA.module',
    data: {preload: true}
  },
  {
    path: 'moduleB',
    loadChildren: './moduleB.module'
  }
]
```

We start with creating a custom preloading strategy.

```
export class PreloadSelectedModulesList implements PreloadingStrategy {
  preload(route: Route, load: Function): Observable {
    return route.data && route.data.preload ? load() : of(null);
  }
}
```

The `preload` method takes two parameters: a route and the function that actually does the preloading. In it we check if the `preload` property is set to true. And if it is, we call the `load` function.

Finally, we need to enable the strategy by listing it as a provider and passing it to `RouterModule.forRoot`.

```
@NgModule({
  bootstrap: [MailAppCmp],
  providers: [CustomPreloadingStrategy],
  imports: [RouterModule.forRoot(ROUTES,
    {preloadingStrategy: CustomPreloadingStrategy})]
})
class MailModule {}
```

9
Guards

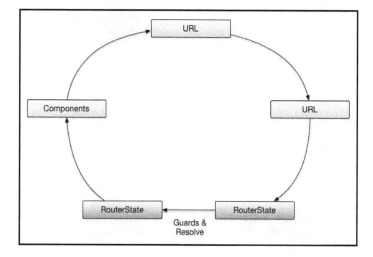

The router uses guards to make sure that navigation is permitted, which can be useful for security, authorization, and monitoring purposes.

There are four types of guards: `canLoad`, `canActivate`, `canActivateChild`, and `canDeactivate`. In this chapter we will look at each of them in detail.

CanLoad

Sometimes, for security reasons, we do not want the user to be able to even see the source code of the lazily loaded bundle if she does not have the right permissions. That's what the `canLoad` guard is for. If a `canLoad` guard returns false, the router will not load the bundle.

Let's take this configuration from the previous chapter and set up a `canLoad` guard to restrict access to contacts:

```
const ROUTES = [
  {
    path: ':folder',
    children: [
      {
        path: '',
        component: ConversationsCmp
      },
      {
        path: ':id',
        component: ConversationCmp,
        children: [...]
      }
    ]
  },
  {
    path: 'contacts',
    canLoad: [CanLoadContacts],
    loadChildren: 'contacts.bundle.js'
  }
];
```

Where the `CanLoadContacts` class is defined like this:

```
@Injectable()
class CanLoadContacts implements CanLoad {
  constructor(private permissions: Permissions,
              private currentUser: UserToken) {}

  canLoad(route: Route): boolean {
    if (route.path === "contacts") {
      return this.permissions.canLoadContacts(this.currentUser);
    } else {
      return false;
    }
  }
}
```

Note that in the configuration preceding the line `canLoad:  [CanLoadContacts]` does not tell the router to instantiate the guard. It instructs the router to fetch `CanLoadContacts` using dependency injection. This means that we have to register `CanLoadContacts` in the list of providers somewhere (for example, when bootstrapping the application):

```
@NgModule({
    //...
    providers: [CanLoadContacts],
    //...
})
class MailModule {
}
platformBrowserDynamic().bootstrapModule(MailModule);
```

The router will use dependency injection to get an instance of `CanLoadContacts`. After that, the route will call the `canLoad` method, which can return a promise, an observable, or a boolean. If the returned value is a promise or an observable, the router will wait for that promise or observable to complete before proceeding with the navigation. If the returned value is false, the navigation will fail. We could also use a function with the same signature instead of the class as shown in the following code:

```
{
    path: 'contacts',
    canLoad: [canLoad],
    loadChildren: 'contacts.bundle.js'
}

function canLoad(route: Route): boolean {
    // ...
}

@NgModule({
    //...
    providers: [{provide: canLoad, useValue: canLoad}],
    //...
})
class MailModule {
}
platformBrowserDynamic().bootstrapModule(MailModule);
```

Finally, the router will call the `canLoad` guard during any navigation loading contacts, not just the first time, even though the bundle itself will be loaded only once.

CanActivate

The `canActivate` guard is the default mechanism of adding permissions to the application. To see how we can use it, let's take the example from preceding code and remove lazy loading:

```
const ROUTES = [
  {
    path: ':folder',
    children: [
      {
        path: '',
        component: ConversationsCmp
      },
      {
        path: ':id',
        component: ConversationCmp,
        children: [...]
      }
    ]
  },
  {
    path: 'contacts',
    canActivate: [CanActivateContacts],
    children: [
      { path: '', component: ContactsCmp },
      { path: ':id', component: ContactCmp }
    ]
  }
];
```

Where `CanActivateContacts` is defined as shown in the following code:

```
@Injectable()
class CanActivateContacts implements CanActivate {
  constructor(private permissions: Permissions,
              private currentUser: UserToken) {}

  canActivate(route: ActivatedRouteSnapshot, state: RouterStateSnapshot):
    boolean {
    if (route.routerConfig.path === "contacts") {
      return this.permissions.canActivate(this.currentUser);
    } else {
      return false;
    }
  }
}
```

```
    }
```

As with `canLoad`, we need to add `CanActivateContacts` to a list of providers, as follows:

```
@NgModule({
    //...
    providers: [CanActivateContacts],
    //...
})
class MailModule {
}
platformBrowserDynamic().bootstrapModule(MailModule);
```

Note, the signatures of the `canLoad` and `canActivate` guards are different. Since `canLoad` is called during the construction of the router state, and `canActivate` is called after, the `canActivate` guard gets more information. It gets its activated route and the whole router state, whereas the `canLoad` guard only gets the route. As with `canLoad`, the router will call `canActivate` any time an activation happens, which includes any parameters' changes.

CanActivateChild

The `canActivateChild` guard is similar to `canActivate`, except that it is called when a child of the route is activated, and not the route itself.

Imagine a function that takes a URL and decides if the current user should be able to navigate to that URL. That means, we would like to check that any navigation is permitted. This is how we can accomplish this by using `canActivateChild`:

```
{
    path: '',
    canActivateChild: [AllowUrl],
    children: [
      {
        path: ':folder',
        children: [
          { path: '', component: ConversationsCmp },
          { path: ':id', component: ConversationCmp, children: [...]}
        ]
      },
      {
        path: 'contacts',
        children: [
          { path: '', component: ContactsCmp },
          { path: ':id', component: ContactCmp }
        ]
```

```
        }
      ]
    }
```

Where `AllowUrl` is defined like this:

```
@Injectable()
 class AllowUrl implements CanActivateChild {
   constructor(private permissions: Permissions,
               private currentUser: UserToken) {}

   canActivate(route: ActivatedRouteSnapshot, state: RouterStateSnapshot):
     boolean {
     return this.permissions.allowUrl(this.currentUser, state.url);
   }
 }
```

Since we placed the guard at the very root of the router configuration, it will be called during any navigation.

CanDeactivate

The `canDeactivate` guard is different from the rest. Its main purpose is not to check permissions, but to ask for confirmation.

To illustrate this let's change the application to ask for confirmation when the user closes the compose dialog with unsaved changes:

```
[
    {
      path: 'compose',
      component: ComposeCmp,
      canDeactivate: [SaveChangesGuard]
      outlet: 'popup'
    }
  ]
```

Where `SaveChangesGuard` is defined as follows:

```
class SaveChangesGuard implements CanDeactivate<ComposeCmp> {
    constructor(private dialogs: Dialogs) {}

    canDeactivate(component: ComposeCmp, route: ActivatedRouteSnapshot,
                  state: RouterStateSnapshot): Promise<boolean> {
        if (component.unsavedChanges) {
            return this.dialogs.unsavedChangesConfirmationDialog();
        } else {
            return Promise.resolve(true);
        }
    }
}
```

The `SaveChangesGuard` class asks the user to confirm the navigation because all the unsaved changes would be lost. If she confirms, the `unsavedChangesConfirmationDialog` will return false, and the navigation will be cancelled.

10
Events

The router provides an observable of navigation events. Any time the user navigates somewhere, or an error is thrown, a new event is emitted. This can be useful for setting up monitoring, troubleshooting issues, implementing error handling and so on.

Enable tracing

The very first thing we can do during development to start troubleshooting router-related issues is to enable tracing, which will print out every single event in the console.

```
@NgModule({
  import: [RouterModule.forRoot(routes, {enableTracing: true})]
})
class MailModule {
}
platformBrowserDynamic().bootstrapModule(MailModule);
```

Listening to events

To listen to events, inject the router service and subscribe to the events observable.

```
class MailAppCmp {
  constructor(r: Router) {
    r.events.subscribe(e => {
      console.log("event", e);
    });
  }
}
```

For instance, let's say we want to update the title any time the user successfully navigates. An easy way to do that would be to listen to all NavigationEnd events:

```
class MailAppCmp {
  constructor(r: Router, titleService: TitleService) {
    r.events.filter(e => e instanceof NavigationEnd).subscribe(e => {
      titleService.updateTitleForUrl(e.url);
    });
  }
}
```

Grouping by navigation ID

The router assigns a unique ID to every navigation, which we can use to correlate events. Perform the following steps.

1. Let's start with defining a few helpers used for identifying the start and the end of a particular navigation:

```
function isStart(e: Event): boolean {
  return e instanceof NavigationStart;
}

function isEnd(e: Event): boolean {
  return e instanceof NavigationEnd ||
         e instanceof NavigationCancel ||
         e instanceof NavigationError;
}
```

2. Next, let's define a combinator that will take an observable of all the events related to a navigation and reduce them into an array:

```
function collectAllEventsForNavigation(obs: Observable):
  Observable<Event[]>{
  let observer: Observer<Event[]>;
  const events = [];
  const sub = obs.subscribe(e => {
    events.push(e);
    if (isEnd(e)) {
      observer.next(events);
      observer.complete();
    }
  });
  return new Observable<Event[]>(o => observer = o);
}
```

3. Now equipped with these helpers, we can implement the desired functionality as follows:

```
class MailAppCmp {
  constructor(r: Router) {
    r.events.

      // Groups all events by id and returns Observable<Observable<Event>>.
      groupBy(e => e.id).

      // Reduces events and returns Observable<Observable<Event[]>>.
      // The inner observable has only one element.
      map(collectAllEventsForNavigation).

      // Returns Observable<Event[]>.
      mergeAll().

      subscribe((es:Event[]) => {
        console.log("navigation events", es);
      });
  }
}
```

Showing spinner

In the last example let's use the events observable to show the spinner during navigation:

```
class MailAppCmp {
  constructor(r: Router, spinner: SpinnerService) {
    r.events.
      // Fitlers only starts and ends.
      filter(e => isStart(e) || isEnd(e)).

      // Returns Observable<boolean>.
      map(e => isStart(e)).

      // Skips duplicates, so two 'true' values are never emitted in a row.
      distinctUntilChanged().

      subscribe(showSpinner => {
        if (showSpinner) {
          spinner.show();
        } else {
          spinner.hide();
        }
      });
  }
}
```

11
Testing Router

Everything in Angular is testable, and the router isn't an exception. In this chapter we will look at three ways to test routable components: isolated tests, shallow tests, and integration tests.

Isolated tests

It is often useful to test complex components without rendering them. To see how it can be done, let's write a test for the following component:

```
@Component({moduleId: module.id, templateUrl: 'compose.html'})
class ComposeCmp {
  form = new FormGroup({
    title: new FormControl('', Validators.required),
    body: new FormControl('')
  });

  constructor(private route: ActivatedRoute,
              private currentTime: CurrentTime,
              private actions: Actions) {}

  onSubmit() {
    const routerStateRoot = this.route.snapshot.root;
    const conversationRoute = routerStateRoot.firstChild;
    const conversationId = +conversationRoute.params['id'];

    const payload = Object.assign({},
      this.form.value,
      {createdAt: this.currentTime()});

    this.actions.next({
      type: 'reply',
```

```
      conversationId: conversationId,
      payload: payload
    });
  }
}
```

Here's the `compose.html` file:

```html
<form [formGroup]="form" (ngSubmit)="onSubmit()">
  <div>
    Title: <md-input formControlName="title" required></md-input>
    <span *ngIf="form.get('title').touched &&
      form.hasError('required', 'title')">
      required
    </span>
  </div>
  <div>
    Body: <textarea formControlName="body"></textarea>
  </div>
  <button type="submit" [disabled]="form.invalid">Reply</button>
</form>
```

There a few things in this example worth noting:

- We are using reactive forms in the template of this component. This require us to manually create a `form` object in the `component` class, which has a nice consequence: we can test input handling without rendering the template.
- Instead of modifying any state directly, `ComposeCmp` emits an action, which is processed elsewhere. Thus the isolated test will have to only check that the action has been emitted.
- The `this.route.snapshot.root` returns the root of the router state, and `routerStateRoot.firstChild` gives us the conversation route to read the `id` parameter from.

Now, let's look at the following test:

```javascript
describe('ComposeCmp', () => {
  let actions: BehaviorSubject;
  let time: CurrentTime;

  beforeEach(() => {
    // this subject acts as a "spy"
    actions = new BehaviorSubject(null);

    // dummy implementation of CurrentTime
    time = () => '2016-08-19 9:10AM';
```

```
  });

  it('emits a reply action on submit', () => {
    // a fake activated route
    const route = {
      snapshot: {
        root: {
          firstChild: { params: { id: 11 } }
        }
      }
    };
    const c = new ComposeCmp(route, time, actions);

    // performing an action
    c.form.setValue({
      title: 'Categorical Imperative vs Utilitarianism',
      body: 'What is more practical in day-to-day life?'
    });
    c.onSubmit();

    // reading the emitted value from the subject
    // to make sure it matches our expectations
    expect(actions.value.conversationId).toEqual(11);
    expect(actions.value.payload).toEqual({
      title: 'Categorical Imperative vs Utilitarianism',
      body: 'What is more practical in day-to-day life?',
      createdAt: '2016-08-19 9:10AM'
    });
  });
});
```

As you can see, testing routable Angular components in isolation is no different from testing any other JavaScript object.

Shallow testing

Testing component classes without rendering their templates works in certain scenarios, but not in all of them. Sometimes we can write a meaningful test only if we render a component's template. We can do that and still keep the test isolated. We just need to render the template without rendering the component's children. This is what is colloquially known as shallow testing.

Let's see this approach in action in the following code:

```
@Component(
    {moduleId: module.id, templateUrl: 'conversations.html'})
export class ConversationsCmp {
  folder: Observable<string>;
  conversations: Observable<Conversation[]>;

  constructor(route: ActivatedRoute) {
    this.folder = route.params.pluck<string>('folder');
    this.conversations = route.data.pluck<Conversation[]>('conversations');
  }
}
```

This constructor, although short, may look a bit funky if you are not familiar with RxJS. So let's step through it. First, we pluck `folder` out of the `params` object, which is equivalent to `route.params.map(p => p['folder'])`. Second, we pluck out conversations.

In the template we use the async pipe to bind the two observables. The async pipe always returns the latest value emitted by the following observable:

```
{{folder|async}}

<md-card *ngFor="let c of conversations|async" [routerLink]="[c.id]">
    <h3>
      <a [routerLink]="[c.id]">{{c.title}}</a>
    </h3>
    <p>
      <span class="light">{{c.user.name}} [{{c.user.email}}]</span>
    </p>
  </md-card>
```

Now let's look at the test in the following code:

```
describe('ConversationsCmp', () => {
    let params: BehaviorSubject<string>;
    let data: BehaviorSubject<any>;

    beforeEach(async(() => {
      params = of({
        folder: 'inbox'
      });

      data = of({
        conversations: [
          {
            id: 1,
            title: 'On the Genealogy of Morals by Nietzsche',
```

```
          user: {name: 'Kate', email: 'katez@example.com'}
        },
        {
          id: 2,
          title: 'Ethics by Spinoza',
          user: {name: 'Corin', email: 'corin@example.com'}
        }
      ]
    });

    TestBed.configureTestingModule({
      declarations: [ConversationsCmp],
      providers: [
        { provide: ActivatedRoute, useValue: {params, data} }
      ]
    });
    TestBed.compileComponents();
  }));

  it('updates the list of conversations', () => {
    const f = TestBed.createComponent(ConversationsCmp);
    f.detectChanges();

    expect(f.debugElement.nativeElement).toHaveText('inbox');
    expect(f.debugElement.nativeElement).toHaveText('On the Genealogy of
Morals');
    expect(f.debugElement.nativeElement).toHaveText('Ethics');

    params.next({
      folder: 'drafts'
    });

    data.next({
      conversations: [
        { id: 3, title: 'Fear and Trembling by Kierkegaard', user: {name:
'Someone
        Else', email: 'someonelse@example.com'} }
      ]
    });
    f.detectChanges();

    expect(f.debugElement.nativeElement).toHaveText('drafts');
    expect(f.debugElement.nativeElement).toHaveText('Fear and Trembling');
  });
});
```

First, look at how we configured our testing module. We only declared
ConversationsCmp, nothing else. This means that all the elements in the template will be
treated as simple DOM nodes, and only common directives (for example: ngIf and ngFor)
will be applied. This is exactly what we want. Second, instead of using a real activated
route, we are using a fake one, which is just an object with the params and data properties.

Integration testing

Finally, we can always write an integration test that will exercise the whole application, as
shown in the following code:

```
describe('integration specs', () => {
   const initialData = {
      conversations: [
         {id: 1, title: 'The Myth of Sisyphus'},
         {id: 2, title: 'The Nicomachean Ethics'}
      ],
      messages: [
         {id: 1, conversationId: 1, text: 'The Path of the Absurd Man'}
      ]
   };

   beforeEach(async(() => {
     TestBed.configureTestingModule({
        // MailModule is an NgModule that contains all application
        // components and the router configuration

        // RouterTestingModule overrides the router and location providers
        // to make them test-friendly.
        imports: [MailModule, RouterTestingModule],

        providers: [
           { provide: 'initialData', useValue: initialData}
        ]
     });
     TestBed.compileComponents();
   }));

   it('should navigate to a conversation', fakeAsync(() => {
     // get the router from the testing NgModule
     const router = TestBed.get(Router);

     // get the location from the testing NgModule,
     // which is a SpyLocation that comes from RouterTestingModule
     const location = TestBed.get(Location);
```

```
    // compile the root component of the app
    const f = TestBed.createComponent(MailAppCmp);

    router.navigateByUrl("/inbox");
    advance(f);

    expect(f.debugElement.nativeElement).toHaveText('The Myth of
Sisyphus');
    expect(f.debugElement.nativeElement).toHaveText('The Nicomachean
Ethics');

    // find the link
    const c = f.debugElement.query(e => e.nativeElement.textContent ===
"The Myth of
    Sisyphus");
    c.nativeElement.click();
    advance(f);

    expect(location.path()).toEqual("/inbox/0");
    expect(f.nativeElement).toHaveText('The Path of the Absurd Man');
  }));
});

function advance(f: ComponentFixture<any>) {
  tick();
  f.detectChanges();
}
```

Even though both the shallow and integration tests render components, these tests are very different in nature. In the shallow test we mocked up every single dependency of a component. In the integration one we did it only with the location service. Shallow tests are isolated, and, as a result, can be used to drive the design of our components. Integration tests are only used to check the correctness.

Summary

In this chapter we looked at three ways to test Angular components: isolated tests, shallow tests, and integration tests. Each of them have their time and place: isolated tests are a great way to test drive your components and test complex logic. Shallow tests are isolated tests on steroids, and they should be used when writing a meaningful test requires to render a component's template. Finally, integration tests verify that a group of components and services (for example: the router) work together.

12
Configuration

In this last chapter we will look at configuring the router.

Importing RouterModule

We configure the router by importing RouterModule, and there are two ways to do it: `RouterModule.forRoot` and `RouterModule.forChild`.

`RouterModule.forRoot` creates a module that contains all the router directives, the given routes, and the router service itself. And `RouterModule.forChild` creates a module that contains all the directives and the given routes, but does not include the service.

The router library provides two ways to configure the module because it deals with a shared mutable resource—location. That is why we cannot have more than one router service active—they would clobber each other. Therefore we can use `forChild` to configure every lazy-loaded child module, and `forRoot` at the root of the `application`. `forChild` can be called multiple times, whereas `forRoot` can be called only once.

```
@NgModule({
    imports: [RouterModule.forRoot(ROUTES)]
})
class MailModule {}

@NgModule({
    imports: [RouterModule.forChild(ROUTES)]
})
class ContactsModule {}
```

Configuring router service

We can configure the router service by passing the following options to
`RouterModule.forRoot`:

- The `enableTracing` option makes the router log all its internal events to the console
- The `useHash` option enables the location strategy that uses the URL fragment instead of the history API
- The `initialNavigation` option disables the initial navigation
- The `errorHandler` option provides a custom error handler

Let's look at each of them in detail.

Enable tracing

Setting `enableTracing` to `true` is a great way to learn how the router works as shown in the following code:

```
@NgModule({
    imports: [RouterModule.forRoot(ROUTES, {enableTracing: true})]
})
class MailModule {}
```

With this option set, the router will log every internal event to the your console. You'll see something like the following code:

```
Router Event: NavigationStart
 NavigationStart(id: 1, url: '/inbox')

Router Event: RoutesRecognized
RoutesRecognized(id: 1, url: '/inbox', urlAfterRedirects: '/inbox', state:
  Route(url:'', path:'') {
    Route(url:'inbox', path:':folder') {
      Route(url:'', path:'')
    }
  }
)

Router Event: NavigationEnd
 NavigationEnd(id: 1, url: '/inbox', urlAfterRedirects: '/inbox')
```

```
Router Event: NavigationStart
NavigationStart(id: 2, url: '/inbox/0')

Router Event: RoutesRecognized
RoutesRecognized(id: 2, url: '/inbox/0', urlAfterRedirects: '/inbox/0',
state:
   Route(url:'', path:'') {
     Route(url:'inbox', path:':folder') {
       Route(url:'0', path:':id') {
         Route(url:'', path:'')
       }
     }
   }
)

Router Event: NavigationEnd
NavigationEnd(id: 2, url: '/inbox/0', urlAfterRedirects: '/inbox/0')
```

You can right click on any of the events and store them as global variables. This allows you to interact with them: inspect router state snapshots, URLs, and so on.

Use hash

The router supports two location strategies out of the box: the first one uses the browser history API, and the second one uses the URL fragment or hash. To enable the hash strategy, do the following:

```
@NgModule({
  imports: [RouterModule.forRoot(ROUTES, {useHash: true})]
})
class MailModule {}
```

You can also provide your own custom strategy as follows:

```
@NgModule({
  imports: [RouterModule.forRoot(ROUTES)],
  providers: [{provide: LocationStrategy, useClass:
MyCustomLocationStrategy}]
})
class MailModule {}
```

Disable initial navigation

By default, RouterModule.forRoot will trigger the initial navigation: the router will read the current URL and will navigate to it. We can disable this behavior to have more control.

```
@NgModule({
  imports: [RouterModule.forRoot(ROUTES, {initialNavigation: false})],
})
class MailModule {
  constructor(router: Router) {
    router.navigateByUrl("/fixedUrl");
  }
}
```

Custom error handler

Every navigation will either succeed, will be cancelled, or will error. There are two ways to observe this.

The router.events observable will emit:

- NavigationStart when navigation stars
- NavigationEnd when navigation succeeds
- NavigationCancel when navigation is canceled
- NavigationError when navigation fails

All of them contain the id property we can use to group the events associated with a particular navigation.

If we call router.navigate or router.navigateByUrl directly, we will get a promise that:

- will be resolved with true if the navigation succeeds
- will be resolved with false if the navigation gets cancelled
- will be rejected if the navigation fails

Navigation fails when the router cannot match the URL or an exception is thrown during the navigation. Usually this indicates a bug in the application, so failing is the right strategy, but not always. We can provide a custom error handler to recover from certain errors as shown in the following code:

```
function treatCertainErrorsAsCancelations(error) {
    if (error isntanceof CancelException) {
      return false; //cancelation
    } else {
      throw error;
    }
}

@NgModule({
    imports: [RouterModule.forRoot(ROUTES, {errorHandler:
treatCertainErrorsAsCancelations})]
  })
  class MailModule {}
```

Fin

This is the end of this short book on the Angular Router. We have learned a lot. We looked at what routers do in general: they are responsible for manage state transitions. Then we looked at the Angular router: its mental model, its API, and the design principles behind it. We also learned how to test applications using the router, and how to configure it.

Bug reports

If you find any typos, or have suggestions on how to improve the book, please, email me at `avix1000@gmail.com`.

Example app

Throughout the book I used the same application in all the examples. You can find the source code of this application here: `https://github.com/vsavkin/router_mailapp MailApp`.

Index

www.ingramcontent.com/pod-product-compliance
Lightning Source LLC
Chambersburg PA
CBHW060156060326
40690CB00018B/4139